Y0-BZB-238

Toby

THE TABBY KITTEN

Toby

THE TABBY KITTEN

Text and photographs by

COLLEEN STANLEY BARE

COBBLEHILL BOOKS / Dutton   New York

To Michael

Library of Congress Cataloging-in-Publication Data

Bare, Colleen Stanley.
    Toby the tabby kitten / text and photographs by Colleen Stanley Bare.
        p.   cm.
    ISBN 0-525-65211-6
    1. Manx cat—Juvenile literature.   2. Kittens—Juvenile literature.
3. Cats—Juvenile literature.   [1. Manx cat.   2. Cats.]   I. Title.
SF449.M36B37   1995
636.8'23—dc20   94-42912   CIP   AC

Published in the United States by Cobblehill Books,
an affiliate of Dutton Children's Books,
a division of Penguin Books USA Inc.
375 Hudson Street, New York, New York 10014

Designed by Charlotte Staub
Printed in Hong Kong   First Edition
10 9 8 7 6 5 4 3 2 1

This is the story of Toby, a baby tabby cat.
He looks like an ordinary striped tabby kitty —
except for an unordinary difference.
Toby doesn't have a tail.

He doesn't have a tail,
because he is a breed of cat called Manx.
Many Manx cats are born without tails.

Toby belongs to a girl named Sarah. Or rather,
Sarah belongs to a kitten named Toby.

Toby also owns Sarah's dog, a labrador called Duke.

Toby plays
with Duke's nose.

He plays
with Duke's tail.

Sarah talks to Toby.
She holds him and tells him about her day.
He seems to listen and purrs.

Toby talks to Sarah.
When Sarah talks, she speaks English.
When Toby talks, he speaks Cat.
His cat talk is mostly meow talk, such as his
"Feed me now" meow. He also meows,
"Let me in, let me out,
pick me up, put me down, stroke my back,
let me nap on your lap — *now!*"

Toby makes other sounds.
He yowls when he gets hurt.
He growls when he is angry.
He hisses when he is scared.

Toby uses his sharp senses to try to catch mice.
He has superhearing, even better than Duke's.
He can hear extra high-pitched sounds —
mouse squeaks, bird chirps, cat mews.
Each ear can move separately,
to pick up noises from
different directions.

He has supereyesight.

He can see at least six times better
than you can see at night.
This helps him hunt mice. The pupils
of his eyes become large in dim
light, narrow in bright light.

Toby's supersmelling sense tells him where mice
are hiding, such as in a woodpile.
His whiskers are important to his touching sense.
They are the feelers that guide him through
tight places in a woodpile.

Toby has four padded paws with eighteen toes —
five on each front foot and four on the back.
A needle-sharp claw is at the end of each toe,
which he can push out for scratching,
climbing, and grabbing.
He scratches his claws against tree bark, fences,
and sometimes carpets and chairs.
OOPS! Toby is in trouble.

Toby is a playcat.

He plays with
cat toys.

He plays with
a broom.

He plays with
string.

13

His playing teaches him grown-up lessons.
He pounces and grabs, as at a mouse.
He swats and pokes, as at a bird.
He chases, as after mice and other cats.

Toby likes to hide. When Sarah calls, "Come, Toby,"
he sometimes stays hidden.
He hides in a paper bag.

He hides in the tulips. Can you find Toby?

The first time Toby tries to climb a tree,
he looks scared. He goes a few feet up the trunk
of a big oak tree. He stops and digs
his claws into the bark.
He hangs on, looking down. Help!
He jumps to the ground.

Toby finds a smaller tree.
He runs up the trunk, then stops to chew.
He chews on slender soft branches, on tender
tasty leaves, on pieces of bark.

Toby rests on a branch. He seems to be thinking,
"What shall I do now?"
Finally, he backs down *very* carefully.

Toby's favorite food
would be mouse, if he could catch any.
So far, the crafty mice have been quicker than Toby.
He settles for all-day snacking on crunchy kitty
kibble and canned kitten food dinners.
Soon he will lose his baby teeth and, by six months,
will have thirty grown-up ones.
Then, watch out mice!

He sneaks a lick from Sarah's ice-cream cone.

Toby has his own water dish.
He curves his pink tongue into a spoon shape
and laps without spilling.

He sleeps in his basket bed and grooms between naps.
Like all cats, he snoozes about sixteen hours
a day. He seems to dream.

Toby is self-cleaning.
Several times a day he washes and
cleans his fur with his long limber tongue.
The tongue is like sandpaper, covered with many
tiny hooks. It works like a comb on his fur.

He washes his face by first licking a front paw.
Then he uses the wet paw as a washcloth,
rubbing it around his face, ears, and head.
He washes everything he can reach:
paws, legs, stomach, right side, left side.

Toby's coat gets a human brushing
at least once a week.

One day Sarah takes Toby to visit school.
He rides in a carrying cage.

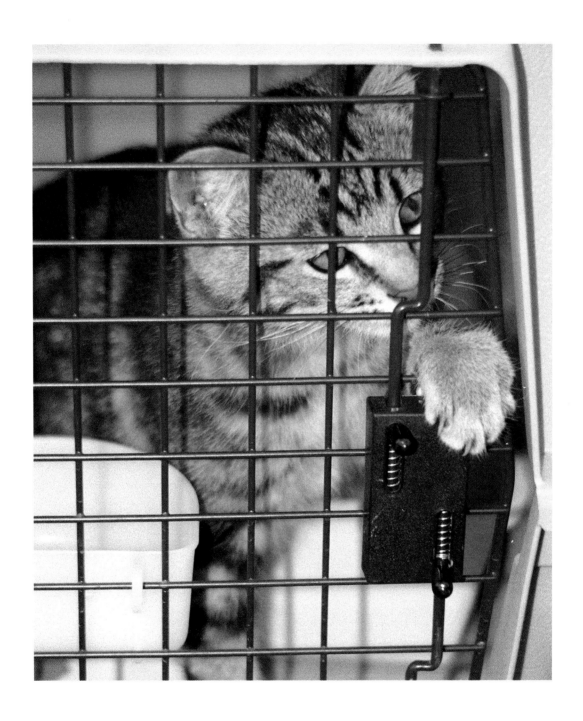

He tries to open the cage door with his paw.
Toby is a smart cat.

At school,
the children gather
around him and
pat his fur.

They hold him and take him down the slide.

By winter, Toby knows every paw step
of his neighborhood. He has found the best
bushes for hiding and the best trees for climbing.
He has learned where to avoid noisy dogs
and crabby cats. He has discovered
a brush pile that smells of mice.
He knows his way home.

Now Toby is almost grown up,
from kitten to cat.

MORE CAT FACTS

Domestic cats are found all over the world, with nearly 60 million just in the United States. These tamed cats are closely related to wildcats and share many traits. Therefore, all cats have been placed in one scientific family called Felidae, which has thirty-five species divided into three groups or genera.

The three groups are: *Panthera*, with six species consisting of the lion, tiger, leopard, jaguar, snow leopard, and clouded leopard; *Acinonyx*, with only the cheetah; and *Felis*, which includes the domestic cat and twenty-seven other species such as the lynx, bobcat, cougar, wildcat, and ocelot.

The domestic cat (*Felis sylvestris catus*) is thought to be a descendent of the small tabbylike African wildcat (*Felis sylvestris lybica*). These cats were tamed about 2000 B.C. in ancient Egypt and were highly valued for their mice and rat hunting skills.

The Manx breed originated hundreds of years ago on the Isle of Man in the Irish Sea, where thousands of Manx cats still run freely. Only completely tailless Manx cats, called *rumpies*, are accepted for championship competition in cat shows. The Manx taillessness does not seem to interfere with basic cat performance such as climbing and jumping. Manx cats are smart, active, loyal, and playful.

INDEX